You have no normal country
to return to

Also by Tom Sastry:

A Man's House Catches Fire

(Nine Arches Press, 2019)

You have no normal country to return to

Tom Sastry

Nine
Arches
Press

You have no normal country to return to
Tom Sastry

ISBN: 9781913437343
eISBN: 9781913437350

First published April 2022 by:

Nine Arches Press
Unit 14, Sir Frank Whittle Business Centre,
Great Central Way, Rugby.
CV21 3XH
United Kingdom

www.ninearchespress.com

Printed in the United Kingdom by:
Imprint Digital

Nine Arches Press is supported using public funding by Arts Council England.

Supported using public funding by
**ARTS COUNCIL
ENGLAND**

for Carly, Rowan, Mum and Dad

Contents

The crisis consists precisely in the fact that
the old is dying and the new cannot be born;
in this interregnum a great variety of morbid
symptoms appear
   – Antonio Gramsci

My mother gave birth to twins: myself and fear
   – Thomas Hobbes

What will sustain us through the Winter?
Where did last year's lessons go?
Walk me out into the rain and snow
I dream a highway back to you
   – Gillian Welch

A short history of The End of History

i. Be your own witness
The winner of the last news cycle declares eternal victory. All remaining difficulties are local. Your life proceeds in lonely chaos, part of no story bigger than itself. You feel nostalgic for horrors you have never known. On your worst day, you are no-one's cause.

ii. Enchantments collapsing on themselves
Lacking the resources to create their own facts, even dissidents become storytellers. They imagine your life in different ways, find their own moral, throw your truth away. You become a selfish island, the Emperor of your thoughts.

iii. You have no normal country to return to
In their twilight, all British Emperors claim the right to live blamelessly. History must be contained. The first line of defence is 1940. Volunteers patrol the beaches so unauthorised memories cannot land. The second line of defence is the Apocalypse.

Be your own witness

Queen Victoria demands to be made Empress of India

The fingers of the Men of Reason
scratch at their tufts as they speak. When it is decent
I halt them. They retreat in small steps
like careful elephants, and send for younger men

who pour youth and better smiles into the same advice.
Show yourself! they say. If not an Empress
which curiosity would I be? The Most Reclusive Widow?
They have been warned. Their faces bounce back

but fear makes them stupid. For their sake
I am stupid too – until I say they should leave
so at least one wish can be satisfied. My *agitation*
troubles them. They suggest medicine and windows.

It would help if I could ride somewhere impossible:
from peak to peak, across the sea. Each day
before I want him, I want the light as it was.
Later, I crave small rooms: a world I can bear.

Jagannadha

The boy asked for my father's name.
I didn't want him to have it
but couldn't explain why.

He ran to the court
where Dad was playing, shouting
Jag-an-ar-da Jag-an-ar-da

like he now owned a piece of him.
Not just any piece
the one that wasn't mine to give

my clumsy English syllables
naked in a white boy's mouth
proving me false.

My grandparents' names are underwater.
I have no tongue or letters for them.
Taxi drivers will correct me

in the pronunciation of my surname, say
you've never been to India?
as if India was part of my soul.

If it isn't
I am the end of history.
All I begin is myself.

The end of history (1)

after Francis Fukuyama

I heard history was over. I wanted
this to be wrong. I wanted things to turn.
I wanted a world I could find
beautiful on its own, without any
particular good news. I'd never had
a truth that could hold me. So I was glad

when the rage returned, glamorous as nails
bending railings and spitting glass with its
same old ideas. I thought the bombs were love
gone rogue, someone's attempt to shock hope
into life. It worked of course. Hope is back
pitiless as ever, waging war on lack.

The outhouse, 2005

In Sweden, on the island, we found dragonless lakes.
I slipped myself in, a blasphemy
naked and gulping; brown, hairy, and English as toast.

London was bombed by Asian men
with beards and rucksacks. A man
was killed on a tube for matching a description

but I was a red bicycle's mind, clear as roads.
I rested on slimy boulders. When I paused
it was by riding backwards. I slinked home

on pedals, dropped like shots
from their turning bed, botch-mended
and bullied back to our cabin.

There was no need to be kind. We were *happy* then.
We drank whisky for the roar of it.
When the Russian sea moved in, we swam too long

and burned, and puked in the outhouse.
Other times, I sat there; smelt sawdust, sourness and grass
read our host's collection of English euphemisms

smallest room; closet; facilities. I loved the prose of it
called it the seat of consciousness.
I rode two hundred miles, swam, shat, slept.

Three lions

I flinched from the ball, a foreigner's error.
The boy who spat on me was *brave*. He ran towards
the smell of blood. It was the age of Terror.
Ministers condemned it, used the word *cowards*.
Their worst insult: proof of their rage.

On the last day of my first job, the boss told me
it made him puke to have to give me a reference
so I could waste someone else's time. At least he
had the guts to say it. That was his defence.
Not hurting me more was his crime.

I've been brave – important where I couldn't be strong.
Made myself powerful, proud, and not sorry
used indignant words to show someone was wrong.
I sounded ridiculous. I was lucky.
I've met the men I tried to become.

Two tigers

In an Oxford college bedroom
this prince of a young republic
alumnus of a grand colonial school
tells me I don't know my own history
how his grandfather helped break an empire.

British mirrors lie
I see myself in them, distorted

I, a nobody of the diaspora
tell him about growing up
half-foreigner, half-native
in a frightened country
that wants to keep the world out.

I can't become myself
by sending my rulers back. Even so

he does not think my unspoken agreement
to avoid politics with a bigot's sister
is how the future is made.
He thinks the answer is honesty
and reparations.

The next century is my home.
Two tigers sleep on the floor.

The world's history with Britain.
England's dream of itself.

United Kingdom

Is. Your. Mother. English? demands the Welsh girl
who seems to like my tall white friend.
It is a bad moment to discover how angry I am.
Born of an English mother. You're English.

She needs an Englishman
to say English things, in an English way
so she can take his complacency
and prove herself better; thus gratified

she can flirt with my English friend
and laugh with her English colleagues
and know what burns inside her and why.
She can flame in the abstract and warm in the flesh

but not to me. If I am to be
her Englishman, she will be my white girl
ignorant and not bothered by it.
Our companions

who don't realise our quarrel is partly with them
are entertained by her passion
as she performs the ritual of her contempt
the curses and the tossed drink

which she knows
draw every eye in the bar
disciplining me with the threat
of male British violence.

Dual heritage

History is the mirror in which I see myself
the whirling sky on my own horizon.

Carried once, on a groaning litter
into my distant grandparents' lives

there was nothing final I did not bring
not famine, war, disease nor death

now I'm back: a dizzy tourist
with a white-skinned family and hilarious vowels.

I stay in hotels, am driven and flattered
made comfortable, shown the very best things.

I struggle with accents, try not to show it.
Never ask questions, rigid with shame.

At home with the first Gulf War

History ended. Hasselhoff sang. Everyone was free.

A year later, the BBC
enjoyed its first postmodern war
giving it its own logo
and showing buildings with targets on
crumbling with people inside.

On our screens it was more a mini-series
than a long-running soap
but there was time for a rumour
that call-up papers were being secretly printed.
Somewhere, there's a future with your name on it.

We all said, if they came for the sixth form
we'd go to Ireland
except the boy who thought our bombs
would bring *civilisation*
and the girl from a country she called *Rhodesia*.

She didn't pretend to believe
babies were being tipped from incubators.
She said you can't be a passenger and protest against the train.
Our lives were built on oil, so we should fight for it
or run to the hills and join some revolution.

We never knew a choice like that. We wanted peace
like our parents looked for a good price at the pump
but even when the oil wells burned
and the dictator's enemies were abandoned
our allowances still bought shoes, records

and sweetened wines to drink in parks
where we cursed the *fascists* who objected
to spent bottles, swearing and dope smoke.
We couldn't see in ourselves
the carelessness that sets the world on fire.

In the stillness of his moment, deciding

The new kid in the fourth year was SAS.
He'd killed three IRA in a Belfast pub.
Although untrue, this was his truth:
who he felt he was. A man. Tooled up

with me trapped in my moment
of seeing him with the gun, and him
in the stillness of his moment, deciding
if I could go on living. The same question

engulfed me last year, like a dropped sky.
I brought him and his gun back into my thoughts –
lived in that pause. The war in his head
inside the war in mine. A little nest of wars.

Politics is over

I cannot write about flowers
when the flowers of my mind are dead.

If the flowers of my mind could live again
I would put them in these poems, with apologies

to anyone who hates my choice:
flowers, over the truth of terrible things.

Finding yourself, again

Sunday is like Heaven but with you in it
unable to feel anything but yourself.

All the people you told yourself you loved
are smiling in the shade of the willow trees.

Your body, at least, is worth greeting.
There's still something about you they know.

You search for your face in the river
its spectrums of gabbling joy

that shuffle the deck of the present
and shatter the dish of the sky.

You imagine yourself as water.
Your friends say they're glad you came.

Almost

The riddle of my identity has been solved
words like
half-caste / unfair of your parents
one of each? / really? / where were you born?

as a student: *discover your roots*
I'd say the colour
is natural / meaning
enough as I am (a prick)

now you / today
change my skin, my voice
ask where *proximity to whiteness*
leaves me in the story

I imagine / as my own.
I almost fall / silent
almost again / roused / an atom
of the world's rage

looking for someone to provoke
to make me
so frightened / I don't feel
please

what makes you / almost?
Tell me. That's how we heal.

Witness

An incoming train ruffles the air.
A hat takes flight and my body responds.

I stretch out a hand and it sticks.
I see a hatless woman smiling

make the right amount of eye contact
return her smile and her hat.

I can hardly believe it happened.
It reminds me of my old idea of myself.

Most days I free ride
on the mysterious abundance of human warmth

someone else to catch the hats
when my head hangs too low to see them

or hold a stranger's drowning thought
with their eyes.

With good luck and good memory
we can unlock ourselves sometimes.

The day after your next good day
be your own witness.

Enchantments collapsing on themselves

Jesus of Bristol

Jesus came to live in St. Werburghs, at the junction of a ley line and an underground river.

One day, in the chip shop queue, he met a woman passing a wedding ring between the fingers of each hand. She had forgotten her purse, so Jesus bought her chips. When she told him there was too much vinegar, he swapped them for his own.

"Let me walk with you" said Jesus, who never believed he was a stranger.

She thanked him for the chips. She was sure he meant well. She preferred to be alone, if he didn't mind.

Jesus apologised and went on his way. Afterwards he thought *when I try to give, do I just take?* He went to one of the dozen Buddhist centres on Gloucester Road for an answer. In the lobby, he met a man who turned his chair and made a show of giving his full attention.

The man's voice was soft and unctuous as unsalted butter. It said "You have told yourself you are The Giver. It has become a compulsion. Let go of your story – and live."

The man was sharing his treasure. He needed Jesus to see its value, so Jesus gave it a go. It didn't go well. You shouldn't get over yourself if you are God in Man. It does strange things to the weather. Also, you get terrible dreams.

It was because of these dreams that Jesus went to the psychoanalyst. The psychoanalyst asked Jesus about his father. Jesus spoke for a long time, in surround sound. The analyst, who was a Freudian, licked his lips with the driest of dry tongues and appeared to take notes.

Then he said "Tell me about your mother". Jesus began to cry, softly at first.

The contract cleaners prepare Flat 64 for the next tenant

Ever since the city council
lifted the ban on dogs in the high rises

it has been rare for corpses
to go undiscovered for long

but the man who said he was God
who may, in some part, be God

lay, for ten days
on his bathroom floor

a scatter of leaflets on the mat
in happy colours

a welcome silence in the lifts
a question asked too late.

They are scouring and bleaching away his clues.
His possibilities dissolve.

Buckets clatter. A woman works
pushing out effort like hope from a lung.

Eventually, the unseen bustle stops.
An unrecognised discomfort

crosses the hallway. We are silent
trying not to squeak in our chairs

counting the regular visitors
capable of witnessing our absence.

A popular history of urban planning

Concrete says
any shape you can dream.

The streets say damp, rubble
rat, wind, rack-rent and fist.

The best view from here is of the future
a sky in a frame on the wall

morning blue or neon-bright
full of pleasuredomes and expressways.

The apartment has doors you can close at will.
Enough space for your thoughts

an inside toilet. A life
without layers: just thin fabric

between you and the room. There is even
hot water. England says *yes*

breathes in the dust that was a ceiling rose
rescues fireplaces for the suburbs

growls, from the new artery
at the sober dawn of its promise

stained, broken, lonely
its own brief surrender to hope.

Cinderella and, by extension, all other stories

Let her do it without a destiny.

Let her do it as the ugly sister.

Let her do it
because it's her fault
when she cannot point her body's jumbled lines
at some dragon of a day.

Let her do it as the pumpkin squats
smug as a moon on the step.

Let her
through a lifetime of midnights
of enchantments collapsing on themselves

do it

again and again.
Let her do it in memory
of love, or the hope of love.

Let her do it with a prince
who knows he is missing something about her
and cannot meet her eye.

Let her age.
Let her do it with bursitis and rheumatism.

Let her sweep it all up.

Then begin.

What's love got to do with it?

I love the kings and queens of England.
Boys urge me to recite their dates

William the first (the conqueror)
ten sixty-six to ten eighty-seven

I never reach the Plantagenets
before they wheel away, laughing.

As a child I am foreign
my strangeness is for others to describe

I am sometimes welcome.
I read books of glory, making sense

of England's solitary millennium
carving it into monarch-sized portions:

George I, though Protestant
spoke German. George III, though mad

did not. Britain beat France for India
in the Seven Years War but carelessly

lost America. Queen Victoria
was loved by all her peoples.

She was particularly fond
of the Isle of Wight.

The moon people explain the stars

The Man In The Earth came here:
a skinless visor in a bouncing sack of bubbles
unbuoyed by slab-boots and scientific theories.

We felt his need and it shocked us
humblebragging in a machine's voice
lugging his breath like property.

He left bags of his waste and a wind-catcher.
He left a terrible curiosity.
It weakened our tie to the ground.

Some called him God, went after him
out into the Great Loom.
They flash their lights in the dark, trying to get home.

A suburban accountant remembers his whipping boy

I tell people I had a brother who went away
and I mean you. I tell them the house
was cruel to him. I say we were friends.
I tell them about the night we stood
on top of the Black Hole Box, under the skylight.
I showed you which house was Joe's.
You asked me what Joe's house was like inside
so I gave you the piece of kitchen roll which Joe's mother
had wrapped around the cake.
I could tell you loved it and I felt like a king.
Do you remember? It had pictures on.
You must have liked them
because when I went up again you showed me
the outlines of rabbits and cups in the stars.
This is hard for me to write
but I think I showed you my space book
so you would know you were wrong
and you cried. I hated you when you cried
I shouted at you to stop but you wouldn't.
I shouted and shouted and I was crying too
so they came up and after a while
they asked if I would like it
if they sent you
away and I said
yes.

I'm sorry.

I have not always had a good life.
I hope you have.

Your brother, Rex.

The Sea of Tranquility

I didn't know what to get the old man
so I took him to the moon. He stood
holding up the line at the top of the steps
looked out and said
There's nothing there
as if he was talking about another place
he had visited before.
I said *Dad. We're here now.*
He pushed his fingerprints
onto the bulb of my shoulder
let me help him down the steps
the needs of his body hidden in his suit.

He was right. The moon was empty.
We scratched at the emptiness
with our dull pretence of wonder.
But when, finally
the Earth rose without us
the loneliness was perfect.
I could not remember why
back home, it feels so angry.

That moment of silence was my gift to him.
When he said *Don't speak*
he snatched it from me
and presented it to himself.
In spite of this
I allowed the magic in
I forgot about myself
until we were back, standing on the step
turning the key on the dead air we had left
and my own absence hit me again

like a great wave
like a decade, all at once
like a wall, over and over.

Nik, backwards

With effort, you lift the blue elephant of my bag
onto my shoulder and usher me out.
Behind you, the PhD who lives to win at eBay
scoops the coffee from your small expensive packets
for the boyfriend you think she hates.
On the outside, I join your father

feeling your fury at his new girlfriend.
He sends money, one of the things you need.
Your mother didn't want to debate the significance
of her own death with you. What did she want?
Did you ask her? I didn't ask you.
My friendship failed. I look further back:

small triangular boats sunk in the Estuary
cry for their feet. You've just moved here.
The flat Essex light shows the wear on you –
faded T-shirt, band name illegible. I want
the fears we can't find words for to be the same.
You're my best witness. You were there

that last Thursday in the bay window of the Iron Horse.
I'm leaving for the job I know I'm wrong for.
We're drunk. Honest without insight. You call me
a loss to philosophy, say I'm now part
of the Annihilation of Meaning. I say yes but
the Search for Meaning Makes Monsters.

Already, I miss you as you were before:
a black swash of bangles, ankhs and silk shirts
androgynous except for your heedlessness
my friends already drowning in your name.
The boy who bought Anthony's can of Fosters
at the station. Nik the Goth. Nik.

Life-changing news

Blame the wings of hypothetical butterflies
for everything. Hold them

under an imaginary wheel. Silence all the crowing
metaphors. Let no domino fall, no one thing

follow another. Throw so many possessions
into a full bath that no movement

has a single cause. Look again at the letter.
Just paper and type. A brief epilogue

to the story of a tree. It makes me
a man baffled by the letters of his name

who invites himself anonymously
to a life he can't accept as his.

Anyone with these thoughts would know
something is wrong but what? Tomorrow

I can wake, in my normal way
oblivious to my body

trusting the day for that pink minute
before the news breaks again.

The silence in the house

It was the same night those guys died on the road.
Dad came home and announced
we were eating together as a family.

I said I was going out, *remember*.
He thrashed the table with his fist
made the fruit bowl dance. We froze

not because we knew what was coming
but because he wasn't like that. Mum said
she would drive me but he snatched her keys

locked himself in the bathroom.
When she banged on the door
nothing came back. She rang Marc

asked if something had happened
hung up, said something about
policemen and their secrets

grabbed a bottle by the throat. *I'm having some.*
Are you? The answer
if you don't want to think is *yes*.

When we heard the news, she said
At least he made sure you weren't on that road.

It could just be a thing she said.
She hated the silence in the house.

May you live

Interesting times, the curse the English
unable to see themselves as interesting
or cursed
attribute to the Chinese

makes itself at home
in our small damp houses.
We look sidelong at our government
of vain disruptors

and wait.
We stockpile toilet paper.
The Caucasians among us
boast of their new Irish passports

acquired *just in case*.
No-one is planning to flee
yet. No-one is moving off grid
yet. No-one is planning to die.

The unimaginable remains unimagined
and we remain housed, fed
working. Right now
other skies are available

ways of thinking are sold openly
there is still time to publish pictures
of our food. Living disappoints
until rotten history unleashes

its most totalitarian idea.
There is no more deferment.
It is all about the living
the seeing, the touching, the noticing.

Summer 1914

The sun is a yellow bruise
on the haze of sticky breath
that coats our skin. We move

like old drunks, slow, grudging
and deep in our own discomfort
towards the river. Its surface

is brown marble. The weir
sucks thin trails of soiled foam
into its disappointed throat.

We don't care. We run
through our hesitations
past our shame, into the shock

of a change; our shrieks
deterring the dogs, who wish
they could be naked as we are.

The beach house and its meaning

You have a case of Serious. It responds
to cocktails. You'll thank me
and if you don't, it won't matter.
Hasn't it been Summer 1914 all our lives?
If the trains built for the beach are heading to the port
isn't it better not to know?
This is no time to look
at young men, good horses
or anything that has a foot on the world
and think dark, prophetic thoughts.
Allow them the present. They will never need it more.
You may as well tell a dog it's time to live alone.

West Doggerland

I grew up by the sea. My eye traced the slow
distant curve of the world, guessing at
the dark marvels underneath. Soon I knew them:
our smudged-out cities. London. Norwich. Hull.

The water had its victory but we kept
the old maps. One day we'd drain the land
sacrifice fisheries, nurse back soil
spiked with sea-salt, welcome old rivers home.

We soon learnt our limits. Keep dry and store
food for the winter. Saltmarshes became
straits. We stopped wading, took to our boats.
Distances became real. Our language split.

Cack-handed in a world of craft and brawn
I offer stories of my lost homeland
in the style of myth. I tell each island
our flame still burns here. And so I eat.

...This Is Our Story

i.

The moon tour always arrives
in time to watch Earth rise, and leaves
before it's sunk in space.
How much loss can the people face?
There are no inwardly unremarkable lives.

ii.

The future is your own country
stripped of illusions, the cold
average of human fate, an unscripted
hail of events. What will your country do
to make it make sense?

iii.

If a Home Secretary signs my exile
and I'm not told
where, in that moment, am I really from?
Meanwhile, should I take more care
or be, already, what I might become?

iv.

Your colleague says *Eat clean! Stay thin!*
Other people's bets can kill.
This time it's mild! they say, again.
To school a child you go all-in.
They rake your stake: lungs, kidneys, brain.

v.

The dead refuse their names, sick of glory.
Our leaders aren't impressed, arrest
a number in a ghostly raid
have the rest displayed
in the shadow of their phrase...

The history of cosmology

You tacked the heavens with glue
and glittered them with stars
shaking off the excess. The paper wrinkled
but we smoothed it as best
we could. I sliced
a moon from foil and we
pressed it down. We drew a tiny cross
for me and a smaller one for you.
I asked what you could see

and straight off, you found constellations:
the bed and the beach. Around us
were boxes not even unpacked
from the last move. We pushed aside
the sheet on the window. It came off
in your hand. Outside
there were no stars, or they weren't as good.

Interlude

Alternate weekends during lockdown

What have you been up to? I say and Rowan says
watching paint dry. I ask if it's the same paint
as last week. They roll their eyes. It's the same
every week. We play cards. Squares of light fall

from the window, warming the floor for the cat.
We give the cat a voice, a New York accent
to make her sound demanding. Her head turns.
We laugh. Half an eye protests. She leaves.

The squares stretch into diamonds, cross the room.
Rowan says it's *like a sundial.* This makes me proud.

I complete the thought: *except the light moves
against the shade.* I pause. *On good days.*

They know this means something, won't let it go
so we talk. You can't feel nothing forever.

You can't feel your hair because
it feels for itself

My hair says I never understood its sense of humour.
It asks if I remember

how it gags on brisk fingers and cheap shampoo
how it saw me look at hats and said it was scared of the dark
how the woman who cut it short said
she was sorry to do it because it could have been beautiful.

Anyway, they will soon close the barbers.
There'll be no clippers to buy and what will I do then?
My hair has started calling me Einstein.
It hopes for a wild old age with me.

It's 3am. I am noticing the world.
Ambulances pass one by one.
People make lists of their isolation needs.
My hair is insisting on itself

scribbling across the lines of my self-image
muttering about me in the hard voice I taught it.
The room is full of these stories: the hopeful boots
the jobsworth clock. Empathy runs wild.

If you are reading this, I am still alive

In a few days I may have lost interest
in anything but my own suffering

and from that self-pity I may never
emerge. I may be frantic about the will

no-one can safely witness and the gap
between what is known of my affections

and their true extent. More likely
this is hayfever, and this poem similar

to a video made by a fringe politician
in case they are assassinated.

My message to you, from beyond hypochondria
is that I hope my embarrassment

brings you as much joy as it brings me.
It is wonderful to feel my cheeks burn

my body crease again. Thank you
for the beautiful discomfort of your complicated

friendship. Please join me at my dignity's
wake. I will not make a speech.

What if I invite my friends to sit in my garden?

What if, passing through the house
they touch the walls?
What if their breath
is droplet-rich and cloudlike?
What if their saliva coats a glass
and I touch the rim when washing it?
What if they kiss the cats?
What if their arms extend
one high, one low
for me to walk into?
What if I surrender my numbness
and my small hairs spread rumours of touch everywhere?
What if I love them for being here
in a way I can't explain?
What if I get drunk
and try to explain
and this is the wrong thing to do?

A bad year for wasps

March: everything locked down. Water trickled in.

June felt safer. We had the roof fixed
blocking its secret channels.

Above our heads, wasps
began to die.

A swarm of shadows expired
on the window that looks into the loft
blacking out the upward sky
keeping our eyes indoors.

We had our own plague to fear
or we would have called Mike
Field Marshal of the Baited Traps

who says each nest he destroys
is a lost civilisation. Instead
we imagined him:
don't interrupt your enemy
when she is making a mistake.

In the weeks after Christmas
as our fellow subjects died
we noticed the wasps had gone.

The window was stained but clear.

The winter sun came through the skylight
lit our lucky footsteps on the stairs.

Time, the devourer of wasps
kept passing us by.

Sharing a small space

You are asked not to say *beautiful* out loud
because you always do, and your companion
needs no reminder to live through her senses –
doesn't know the difficulty. After that

the view doesn't register, the world tightens
around your mood. You swear off the old joke
which reminds you of laughter, and anecdotes
that bring people to mind. You banish

earworms and stop dad-dancing in the hall.
You are now less irritating and you listen more.
Your voice matters. It speaks, never just
brings into the present something only you need.

The hope is your improved people-skills
will make you less lonely, easier to keep
loving. For now, your head is a kettle
of silence, words condensing on the sides.

The path through the hospital grounds

Everything your teachers said about observation
is wrong. The birds on the roof don't matter
nor the snowdrops, the large windows.

The picture hides the story. This is where
statistics bloom. History's sealed box
where the longest weeks are endured.

Look away now. You have no right
to the old man's pyjamas or his movements.
What you find in the nurse's face, you stole.

There's a reason you are drawn to other people's grief
but you have left the world unfinished.
It matters, selfishly or not.

Take your Armageddon eyes home.
Keep them from the calendar, the mirror.
Of course, the days are full of holes.

How England Dies

It'll be alright says Death. Most say
thank you (we are famously polite)
but fuck off. We still think we're supposed
to save ourselves. We shop hurriedly
make careful meals, wait out the anger
the clapping, the hope. Weeks later
Death comes in the post with an official
letterhead. The Prime Minister calls him
NHS Immunity. With his help
we are beating the world the way we used to.
Death is now too big, too busy for you.
More weeks pass. The government shuts down
except for the Department of Distraction.
Death reappears with news of your
family and friends. You run like a tabloid
quarry. He's everywhere: in the bins
on your phone, your pillow, your lover's lips.
The itch on your face you can't scratch – that's him.
You block him but others share his words.
You hide behind your eyelids. He writes
his story anyway. He has what he needs:
you – wiping your eye with the back
of your hand. Asking for it. Later
he'll ask how you are. Touch your rigid arm.
It'll be alright he'll say. You'll say
thank you (we are famously polite).

You have no normal country to return to

England says yes

You'll know someone like England
who knows what they don't like when they see it.
How they lean over the fence wanting to talk
about people's front gardens, young men
electric scooters, human rights.
How they love your bad news
a plan unravelling, a secret shame.
How they scan your body for signs of woe.
How you mock them and fear them
and are them, sometimes.

You didn't know that, today
England would be out on the street, your street
wearing loud colours and a friendly smile
head tipped back as if to catch the spray
voice fizzing like sorbet
around the delicious word *yes*.

They raise that voice higher *Yes! Yes! Yes!*
You smirk, sensing a joke to be made
about Puritan sex. In that moment
you became England
and they are somewhere brighter
repeating their *yes*
like a prophet or worse, a stranger
so foreign, so frightening, so vague.

The fanatics drag the anchorite from his cell

One heave and he shudders back
into the world; a gibbering crouch of goat-stench
and bird Latin. He gasps, is born
comprehends shame again
hates and fears and is carried through the teeth
of the hole, piping his grief at the people
who buried him.

We make fierce beginnings.
We are breakers of shadows.
Our light is good, not friendly. We hush
the babbling of old wisdom and clear the air
for truth. Walls whiten and windows
gape. Some are blinded.

Mending my thoughts

They started early, a gang of them
digging a hole in the sky above my head
called it *the work*, as Puritans must.

I dared not accuse them of enjoyment
but the way they cheered
as clear, weightless spoil filled my hair

suggested pleasure. The broken stuff
was cold and brittle. I tried to sound
like I knew something. *It's been like that*

for a while I said. The clever one
who gets extra for dealing with the idiot
smiled and talked me through it.

We were both pretending. That night
the starless vacuum pulled at me
so they covered it with a screen

slightly the wrong shade of blue.
It's become part of my Heaven
a home for my clouds.

We will defend our island

by digging a hole, a shelter
where our showreel lights up the dirt
by turning old boasts into scripture

       by guarding old generals in stone
       and common-sensing the spite and the hurt
       by loving ourselves alone

by winning our history in a drawbridge vote
and making less use of the heating
by serving our errors and grounding our boats

       by being what we want to be
       in somebody's silence, repeating
       we are strong, we are good, we are free

Conservatism

My country is exhausted.
It craves boredom, wants to rest
digest its history
live, in the meantime, off its myth

stop its mind racing and dream
its candyfloss dreams, gurgle
ridiculous words, rasp for breath
slop its limbs across a small space

it struggles to share.
Its heart is full of lullabies
and stories which abide by the rule of threes.
For example:

long ago, in its tender age of feeling
whoever loved it most
made it promise to sleep
to restore itself.

The first time, it disobeyed
stepped into the nightmare of its own quarrel
imagined new kinds of freedom
and struck the head from a king.

The second time it cheated the dark
with a longitudinal trick
sailing its share of savage luck
to squat on other people's days.

Finally, its prospects drained
it welcomed its quiet night
and when the night was not quiet
it cursed those who spoke up, wore earplugs.

DDR Museum

At best, they're not worth having. The Trabi
someone waited for, the Young Pioneer's scarf
the crackling fabric samples. We laugh
(glancing at the bug) call them *shabby*.

We're next in line to be revealed as fools
under the future's incredulous eyes.
They'll wonder how we bore it: lived the lies
read those papers, worked the petty rules.

What is our *Sandmännchen*? What will they keep
from England's shame, from being forever wrong –
our liberators with their kind ideas
and well-made things. They'll put the rest to sleep
in a museum. It won't belong
outside it. The life we know. Our fears.

Screening Interview, 2031

Her accent draws me in. She is foreign
and curious, in a way we are not
about each other. So I explain. Then she says
did you think it was enough to be kind?

and I can tell she wants a silence
to demonstrate the power of her question.
I shoot back: *what do you mean by enough?*
because there is no "enough", that's her point.

She pulls a sheaf of pictures from her folder
slides one across the table, says
You could have said no
                    to this.
I pick it up. I can't just leave it there.

She has her silence.
Or this.
Or this.
Can we talk about kindness? she says.

Demolition

something impervious pounding
a soft tinkle of bricks
three dimensions broken on the floor

I am not
this time
the bulldozer

I am the heap
of stricken words
unable to form themselves

Searching for the last word

No-one will tell you that becoming themselves was easy.
We have all escaped from silence to tell the world what silence is like.
We say other people's voices are silencers
because we want them to shut up.
We're testing our rage, to see what it does.
The world shows off its new wounds.
Once in a while
we stop to watch them bleed. Each silent shooter
drops their weapons which fall silently to the floor.
We melt into the crowd, which is to say, into ourselves
still insisting we were bleeding first.
Mostly I read about this on my phone.
I rarely watch TV and when I do
I am shocked at how real it feels with sound.

Last night, a meteorite fell, eleven timezones from here.
One of the continents has gone and we will not see the sun again.
Everyone is shopping.
You can see queues at petrol stations on every channel.
The silent people are visibly upset.
In a few months they will be dead.
Everything on the screen will be archaeology.
Meanwhile, let's drink.
Outside, the last safe rain falls on the still-green earth.
The reporter speaks of the enormity of the disaster for which
     there are no words.
He fears silence more than anything.
The silence he fears most is his own.
Watching him
I remember the times I ran my mouth because I knew
there was only one thing I needed to say, so it seemed fair
to carry on until it was said.
I never found out what that thing was
but I guess it was probably
something ordinary about love.

The end of history (2)

They take you in when history spits you out
don't ask questions. It seems they aren't aware
you might be sceptical about
the giant whose boot made the lake, whose chair
the far cliff is. Everything has a name
with a story to it. The world is flat.
Demons find their boots when you bring shame
on the house. They tell you gently – *don't say that.*

As you remember more it gets harder
to see as they see, be as they are:
explained. But where could your knowledge take them?
You can't share what you've lost, fill their larder
with spice, prove the vastness of a star.
All you bring is madness, to shake them.

Empire (it's everything you think)

the colony was real but the Empire was always
a dream
waiting for its sunset

you are several Empires
you have no normal country to return to

Ghosts are made of grief. Why would they be kind?

1. Five years

You take yourself to the beach because *why not?*
It's been a long time without better reasons.

And there she is

wading backwards out of the sea. At first
her skin looks polished, unreal.

She reverses into the clothes and the smile
she left behind, asks after
the ice cream you never offered.
A boy is still screaming in delighted outrage
about the *naked lady*.
His voice sticks in your head
otherwise you would not dare remember
picking lines of kelp from her hair.

It can't be five years, she laughs
nothing has changed. Your hair is grey
but that's not important.
Her love for you is what it was
something you don't understand. You're the one
with a new smile that covers everything:
the length of the pause, its weight
and your rage, that dog you keep close.

2. Hope spreads

She doesn't follow the news but you read
how it's the same everywhere:
the dead returning, unbothered
telling us we were never so serious
eye-rolling our darkness.

When we complain, the still-bereaved
curse our luck, our ingratitude.
They rise early, place fresh laundered clothes
on the sand, keep vigil
brows knotted by the hard white sun.

Waves of bodies roll in from the deeps
retreating into life. The watchers lean further
into the glare, expecting the one
they'll forgive for laughing off
a long absence. Any moment now.

3. The man who married the sea

She lets you out a mile from the beach
so she can disappear. *Who are you?*

she asked as you leafed through your hanging clothes.
I'm your husband you answered.

This, then she said, holding up the wedding shirt
whose cuffs now flap like starched gulls

unfastened at your wrist. *It's fitting.*
It's too small and you're a clown, darkening

with sweat, walking bow-legged
as your feet flinch in the hard shoes.

Small birds of mirth flitter in your wake.
Shutters click. Curiosity follows you

onto the sand, where you shake off
the tailcoat, the cravat, the prison

of perfect memory; everything
but the plain prose of your nakedness.

Then you walk out, into the flint sea
following the ebb tide until

you're out past the headland and could be
anywhere, anyone new.

Thanks and Acknowledgements

This is a pandemic book. It took shape in the silence.

These poems were not honed in public readings. The opportunity to take them to an open mic for instant validation was not there. I wasn't meeting poets and discussing poems over a coffee or a pint of beer.

I have mostly been a lucky poet, with access to a local writing community. But with this book I had to do what many less fortunate poets have always done – sustain my belief in my work for years, without regular doses of encouragement.

For that reason, I owe a huge debt to those who made time to read and discuss these poems as the book came together. In alphabetical order: Suzannah Evans, Malaika Kegode, Hannah Linden, Stefan Mohamed, Danny Pandolfi; and to all those who reviewed or in any way acknowledged its predecessor. Thank you.

Special thanks to Jane Commane for her wisdom and patience; to Angela Hicken for her help and support and to the wider family of Nine Arches poets.

Thanks also to the editors of the following publications in which versions of these poems have appeared: *The Best of 52* (Nine Arches); *Field Notes on Survival* (Bad Betty Press); *The Interpreter's House; Magma; Poetry Review; Poetry Teignmouth;* Verve Poetry Prize anthology (2022); *Wasafiri;* Winchester Poetry Prize Anthology (2019); the *Writers' Café Magazine*.